A Sloth Cannot Rush

By Clem King

A sloth cannot rush.
It is **not** quick.

A sloth can hang.

And it can swim!

A sloth likes to rest a **lot**.

It likes long naps.

This sloth chomps on a lush plant.

When the sun sets,
sloths come out on a quest
for snacks!

Smells help them look for
what they want.

Sloths have thick fuzz.

They brush the fuzz to check for pests.

This is a sloth moth.

The sloth moth chomps the pests on the sloth's fuzz!

This sloth has a kid.

She loves her little sloth so much!

I wish I could pat a sloth!

It could hang from my neck!

CHECKING FOR MEANING

1. What is something that sloths do not do well? *(Literal)*
2. How do sloth moths help sloths? *(Literal)*
3. Why do you think sloths come out at night? *(Inferential)*

EXTENDING VOCABULARY

chomps	Read the word *chomps*. How many sounds are in *chomps*? What are they? What other words have a similar meaning to *chomps*?
lush	The word *lush* can describe something that is thick and healthy. What is described as lush in the text? What else might you describe as lush?
quest	What is a quest? What might you look for on a quest?

MOVING BEYOND THE TEXT

1. Would you like to pat a sloth? Why?
2. Sloths eat plants. What other animals eat plants? What plants do you like to eat?
3. What other animals can you think of that come out at night?
4. Sloths can swim. What other animals can swim?

SPEED SOUNDS

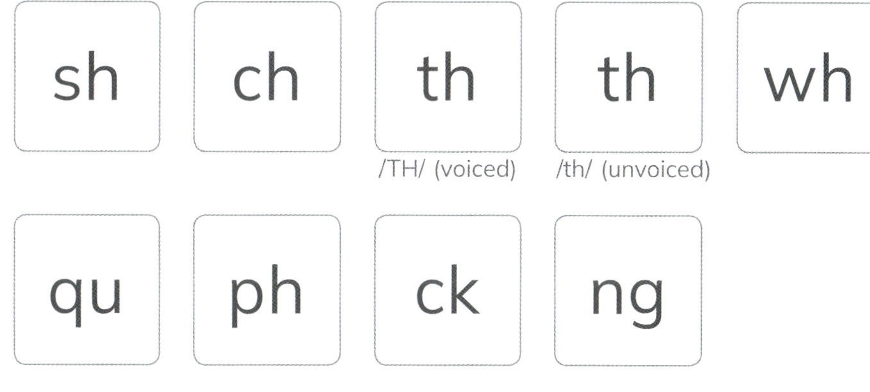

PRACTICE WORDS